BuzzFeed

JOY *in the* STARS

COSMIC JOURNAL

An Astrological Companion
for Health, Happiness,
and Self-Care

**BUZZFEED &
BRIANNE HOGAN**

RP STUDIO

RP Studio™
Hachette Book Group
1290 Avenue of the Americas, New York, NY 10104
www.runningpress.com
@Running_Press

Printed in Singapore

First Edition: September 2021

Published by RP Studio, an imprint of Perseus Books, LLC, a subsidiary of Hachette Book Group, Inc. The RP Studio name and logo is a trademark of the Hachette Book Group.

The publisher is not responsible for websites (or their content) that are not owned by the publisher.

Design by Jason Kayser

ISBN: 978-0-7624-7394-6

COS

10 9 8 7 6 5 4 3 2 1

CONTENTS

INTRODUCTION

Self-care is the ultimate act of self-love. When we implement self-care into our lives, we commit to a routine that nourishes our mental, emotional, spiritual, and physical health. By doing so, we encourage a healthy relationship with ourselves that can radiate to other areas of our life, including our work, our studies, and our bonds with others.

Self-care and self-awareness go hand in hand. When we know ourselves deeply, we can find the path to our most optimal and joyful life. But how do you get to know the real you?

This is where astrology and journaling come in.

Astrology shows us the influence that stars and planets have on our behavior, habits, and character. It's an amazing tool that helps us gain a better understanding of ourselves and how we relate to and interact with the world. Through that understanding, astrology also helps us define our healthy—and unhealthy—habits and can help provide insight into what we need to feel balanced, motivated, happy, and healthy.

Journaling is a powerful self-care tool that promotes self-awareness. Public personalities like Deepak Chopra, Oprah Winfrey, and Jennifer Aniston keep journals. Journaling helps us keep track of our patterns and triggers and can help us explore our deepest fears and dreams. Journaling provides a safe space where we can free our busy mind and deep heart by getting it onto the page.

Together, astrology and journaling can provide insight into your mind, body, soul, and mood to help you live your most joyful and authentic life.

How?

There are twelve zodiac signs, each carrying a certain energy. The vibe that you give off to the world is largely dependent on your sun sign. (There are other factors at play in your birth chart, which is a more comprehensive snapshot of the planets around the sun at the time you were born. Check yours out for a deeper dive into your astrological blueprint.) Understanding your sun sign is usually enough information to give you a personal, authentic guide on how to create and cultivate a happy self-care routine that's perfect for you. Those with a *cusp sign*—someone born toward the end or beginning of a zodiac sign—might feel torn between your sun sign and the following one. In that case, you might want to read both sun signs to glean tips that feel best for your unique energy.

In this journal, you'll get a quick snapshot of your best life according to your zodiac sun sign. Each chapter—mind body, soul, and mood—covers the basics of what you need to know when it comes to self-care: where you struggle and why; journal prompts to help you dig deeper; and the tools, including activities and affirmations, to help you get back to feeling happy.

From avoiding burnout, to helping your body rest, to recognizing emotional triggers and soul-soothing tips, the ultimate goal of this journal is to help you become the best version of you with a little help from the stars.

This journal is a companion to *BuzzFeed Joy in the Stars*, and you're encouraged to read that book to discover even more information about your sign's self-care and self-care suggestions. Use astrology to tune into your authentic and most happy self.

WHAT YOUR SUN SIGN SAYS ABOUT LIVING YOUR BEST LIFE

~~~~~~~~

Find your sun sign in the following pages
to explore what it looks and feels like when you're
living your best, most balanced life.

ARIES

March 21–April 20
The Boss

At your best, Aries, you lead with serious #boss energy, setting the world aflame with dynamism, assertiveness, and an inspiring self-confidence that ignites the fire within those around you. Ruled by Mars, the planet of action and desire, you're a natural leader and creator. You come alive when you're making things happen in the world. Whether you're working on a side hustle, leading a spin class, or planning an epic vacation with your best friends, you feel at your best when you're busy doing projects that electrify you and bring joy to others. It's not a secret that you love running the show. As a fire sign, your electric energy, crystal-clear vision, and dutiful sense of purpose are so hypnotizing that others can't help but flock to your energizing flame.

TAURUS

April 20–May 20
The Sensualist

When you're at your best, Taurus, you're someone who thoroughly enjoys the pleasures of life because you know pleasure is your birthright. You proudly stop to smell the roses. You savor your food and appreciate art. You dance like no one's watching and always ensure that your OOTD is always fire. You take the time to love life. You are ruled by the planet Venus, the planet of love and all things beautiful and pleasurable, so when you practice self-care and self-love, you feel like there's nothing you can't do in life. You view yourself as your own work of art and are committed to creating and carving out the next step in your journey that feels most like your true authentic self: stable, comfortable, and luxurious. As an earth sign, you are deeply inspired by what you see, feel, hear, taste, and touch. And you especially delight in feeling and looking good, #noshame.

GEMINI

May 21–June 20
The Life of the Party

When you're living your best life, Gemini, you are the life of the party.
You're in the zone when you're being your funny, charismatic, and charming
self. Ruled by Mercury, the planet of communication, you're blessed with
the gift of gab, and you have an electric energy that is utterly magnetic.
Mercury also represents intellect, so you have a keen interest in a wide
array of topics, and you never seem to be at a loss for words or information.
As an air sign, you're inherently inquisitive and eat knowledge for break-
fast. You easily become immersed in the latest headlines and find yourself
regularly combing through wormholes of random trivia and facts. You see
your wit and knowledge as the most coveted tools in your arsenal, which
bodes well for you whether you're dating a new love interest or debating a
colleague. Everyone loves this side of you, Gemini, and why wouldn't they?
You're someone who can get along with just about anyone.

CANCER

June 21–July 22
The Nurturer

When you're living your best life, Cancer, you are the hostess with the most-est. Your life is like one big dinner party: you're indulging your interests—like decorating, cooking, and anything related to hearth and home—and creating community. Ruled by the moon, which represents feelings and our greatest needs, you're led by your feelings and instincts. This makes you incredibly intuitive and gifted with an A+ in emotional intelligence. As a water sign, you're naturally sensitive, sensual, and compassionate. You approach your relationships with an open heart and create a feeling of belonging. You're both the nurturer and protector of your inner circle. You gently tend to others' wounds while fiercely guarding them. When you're fully embodying your best self, you trust your gut above facts and figures. You have self-awareness in spades, and you're able to bring out the best in others.

LEO

July 23–August 22
The Showstopper

When you're living your best life, Leo, you command a room like JLo (who shares your sign). You turn heads with your exuberant energy, rockin' body, and fierce confidence. In short, you're a superstar. Ruled by the sun, you've been blessed by the cosmos with a radiant and infectious energy that makes you captivating to watch. A gifted storyteller and performer, you love to be the center of attention. But people don't mind taking a seat and watching you give them the old razzle-dazzle. You have an innate sense to inspire others with your creativity, charm, and cleverness. Represented by the Lion, you're a natural born leader and you attract others with your brave and pioneering aura. As a fire element, you're an innate trailblazer. You're enthusiastic and passionate about creating the life you desire, and your fiery vibe motivates others to do the same. They don't want to just watch you—they want to *be* you.

VIRGO

August 23–September 22
The Organizer

Intelligence meets the divine when you're living your best life, Virgo. Whip smart, and brimming with compassion and a need to help, you're living your best life when you're feeling useful to the world at large. With Mercury, the planet of communication and intellect, as your ruler, you respect knowledge and information, and pride yourself on your ability to communicate with others. Blessed with an analytical mind and as a seeker of truth, you enjoy digging deep on all topics, from life's biggest issues like climate change to personal problems like a friend's breakup. Your passion for diving beneath the surface of life is connected to your commitment to personal growth. As an earth sign, although you're tough on yourself, your goals come from a grounded and practical place. You understand that practice makes perfect, and you won't give up on something until you know you're perfectly skilled at it and can pull it off like no other, like your sign mate, Beyoncé.

LIBRA

September 23–October 22
The Social Butterfly

If there was a zodiac sign that defined love, Libra, that would be you. You love love, and you love to spread love. When you're living your best life, life is one giant love fest. You feel more energized when you are in the presence of others, especially when you're able to make them feel good. It's no surprise, then, that your ruling planet is Venus, the planet of love. You thrive in affectionate and harmonious environments, and you create beauty in all facets of your life. From your wardrobe to your home to how you interact with the world around you, everything about you is striking, graceful, and aesthetically pleasing. As an air sign, you are naturally diplomatic, and you're disconnected enough from your emotions so you can be nonjudgmental and bring logic and intelligence to a disagreement. You're motivated to bridge gaps, mend bridges, and bring everyone into union and harmony. You have a deep understanding and appreciation of what it means to be human, and people feel that when they're within your magnetic energy field.

SCORPIO

October 23–November 21
The Mysterious One

When you're living your best life, Scorpio, you own the fact that you're the most complex yet alluring zodiac sign. Your unique nature is partly due to being ruled by two planets: Mars—the planet of self-expression and action—gives you a passion for life, while Pluto—which represents deep psyche, power, and transformation—allows you to dig deep beneath the surface of it. You are able to see life from a bigger perspective and realize time on earth is precious. As a water sign, feelings are everything to you. You are the embodiment of the phrase "still waters run deep." You're deeply sensitive, empathetic, and intuitive; you just "know" things. Because you feel everything so profoundly, you require a lot of alone time. You like to make meaningful conversation and connections. You don't take life or relationships for granted, which is why you ensure that whatever you're committing to is something that feels authentically right to you on a rich soul level. Everything and anything has meaning to you, Scorpio. In other words, you're deep AF.

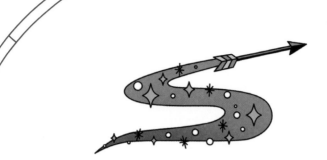

SAGITTARIUS

November 22–December 21
The Adventurer

The world is your playground, Sagittarius, when you're in the zone. Your independent, adventurous, and optimistic energy is on full display as you set out to carve a life that is uniquely yours: unpredictable, free, and full of fun. Ruled by Jupiter, the planet of growth, expansion, and good luck, you're the quintessential free spirit who wants to live your life by your own rules. You're infused by wanderlust and curiosity, and turned off by routine and inertia. As a fire sign, your impulsive and passionate spirit is inspiring as you create your own opportunities and follow your true passions. You have a joyful sense of hope and optimism about the world that's infectious—people love to be in your high-vibe energy. As the aptly named Archer, you're a straight shooter in every sense of the word. You know what you want in life, and you'll do whatever it takes to get it. You not only believe in destiny, but you believe you're destined for greatness.

CAPRICORN

December 22–January 19
The G.O.A.T.

Never mind the boss—when you're in a groove, Capricorn, you're the CEO of
your life. Meaning: You not only get stuff done, but you know how to play the
long game to ensure that your success lasts for a very long time. Ruled by
Saturn, the planet of organization, discipline, and structure, you're all about
following the rules and abiding by a plan. You are symbolized by the Sea
Goat—part goat, part fish. Like the mountain goat, you're willing to take
charge and climb mountains to go after what you want. You rely on tenacity
and a quiet inner strength to move past obstacles and arrive at your destina-
tion, even if it takes you a little longer than most to get there. Blame it on your
earth element. You're methodical, practical, and patient. You know good things
take time, and you're not afraid to wait—and work really hard—for what you
want. You're of the "whatever it takes" mind-set and won't hesitate to put in the
blood, sweat, and tears to be the G.O.A.T.—the Greatest of All Time.

AQUARIUS

January 20–February 18
The Innovator

When you're living your best life, Aquarius, you're changing the world.
Literally. Ruled by Uranus, the planet of rebellion, originality, and revolution, you believe in the power of dynamic change and transformation.
"Out with the old, in with the new!" is your motto. You want to break things
down in order to rebuild, and you're willing to lead the charge. From
participating in pep rallies and social movements to creating new systems
and ways of being at home and work, you're woke AF. As an air sign, you
intellectualize emotions. You're keen on being an objective observer of
life—you want to solve problems and address issues with your logic and
intellect. Your desire for metamorphosis—whether it's for the masses or on
a personal level—is mostly rooted in altruism. You believe in equality and
kindness, and you want everyone, including yourself, to have access to the
same resources and opportunities for a better life. If that means shaking up
the status quo, you'll do whatever it takes.

PISCES

February 19–March 20
The Artist

As the last sign of the zodiac, when you're living your best life, Pisces, you're the embodiment of all the most amazing qualities of the other signs. You're intuitive, creative, compassionate, and healing. Ruled by Neptune, the planet of dreams, inspiration, spirituality, and illusion, you have an otherworldly, almost angelic quality about you. Naturally intuitive, you feel connected to your soul's truth at such a deep level that you will do anything to honor the visions that you've set forth to bring into reality.

As a water sign, you're brimming with a sea of emotion 24/7, which means you're basically a walking sponge for people's feels. Your extreme empathy allows you to connect with others in a way that enables them to be truly seen and appreciated for who they are, and you intuitively understand how to make people feel good. Your powerful imagination coupled with your ability to tap into the deepest of emotions brings an ethereal artistry to everything you do.

MIND

TAKING CARE OF
YOURSELF MENTALLY

~~~~~~~~

When life gets a little stressy and your
mind gets a little messy, look to the stars for
insight and guidance.

ARIES

Sitting still is not an option for the intrepid go-getter that you are. Your intense energy craves challenges and adventures, so you believe that life should always be just that: super challenging and always adventurous. This is why you work on side hustles after your 9-to-5, taking it upon yourself to single-handedly plan a thrilling mountain climbing vacation for you and your friends, or signing up for yet another marathon. Your fiery element gives you a drive like no other, but if you don't keep a well-balanced schedule, your thirst for being on the go 24/7 will inevitably lead to feelings of frustration and being tired AF. It's helpful for you to let your "do do doing" attitude coexist with a sense of "be be being," too.

TAURUS

The true nature of a Taurus is to happily stroll through life. You prefer ease and flow and spending your day merrily indulging your whims. When you're feeling stressed, however, you immediately cling to your comfort zone. The earthy part of you prefers routine and stability in your life because change—whether internal or external—can feel overwhelming to you. As someone who prefers to focus their attention on one thing at a time, you find multitasking impossible when under pressure, and your stubborn nature kicks in as you want to keep things as familiar and easy as possible. For example, if your boss asks you to take on a new responsi-bility you're not prepared for, you'll lie awake all night worried that you might get it "wrong" and wonder how you can get out of it. You're one of the hardest workers of the zodiac, but slipping into a cycle of anxiety can keep you from showing up as your best self, Taurus, and causes you to second guess your worth.

GEMINI

Because your mind is so quick, you have trouble concentrating on even the best of days, Gemini. But when you're not properly taking care of your mental health, your to-do list can become overwhelming, and you might find yourself jumping from one thing to another without finishing anything. When you're not focused on one particular topic, Gemini, your kinetic energy becomes frantic. You easily become distracted with each shiny new thing or person floating into your experience, and your busy mind goes into overdrive. This would be doubly overwhelming for you since you need constant creativity and stimulation. Lackluster jobs, boring assignments, or even the mundane chores of adulting can be mind-numbing experiences for you. As an air sign, your mind and intellect desire titillation 24/7, so you crave spontaneous adventures, new ideas, and creative outlets. Since you despise sitting still and feeling stifled, you could ultimately sabotage yourself by quitting a job or relationship in the name of change.

CANCER

On the outside, you like to show that you have everything together—and perfectly coordinated and curated, of course—but at your core, you often believe you have something to prove. This imbalance stems from a deep-rooted fear of failing to live up to life's expectations and can cause you to feel undervalued and unappreciated. Being a water element and living in your feels make it difficult for you to rationalize your thoughts. When you begin to doubt yourself and/or your ability to cope, you might find yourself going into a spiral that things might never work out for you and that you are categorically and catastrophically stuck. As an intrinsically cautious person who likes their comfort, you find it challenging to take necessary risks to move your life forward. When you're in the depths of despair, it's hard for you to see alternative outcomes that could benefit you. Knowing that you're able to overcome any adversity and refusing to victimize yourself are huge lessons for you, Cancer.

LEO

In a perfect world, Leo, you would spend your days creating projects that make you feel alive. You'd be in your element, running the show, and feeling proud that you're making things happen in the world. Pride is a huge source of validation for you, Leo. You not only like to feel good about yourself, but you also want others to be proud of you, too. The truth is, no matter how confident and certain you appear on the outside, Leo, when your sense of self is imbalanced, you're actually dealing with impostor syndrome on the inside. You question whether you have what it takes to achieve your goals or if you're "enough" to be worthy of them. Your self-esteem plummets, and you doubt your greatness. Why would a courageous Lion like you feel this way? Simple: your ego. On a good day, you have an ego that loves being stroked behind the ears. But when you're feeling overwhelmed and confused with the ins and outs of life and particularly your life's purpose, your ego lets out a mighty growl.

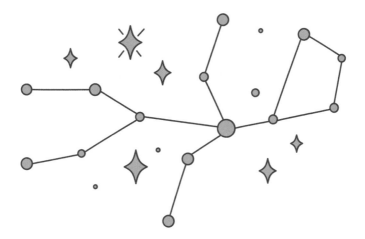

VIRGO

~~~~~~~~~~~~~~~~~~~~~~~~~~~~~~~~~~

You identify as someone of service, Virgo, so you'll load your plate with projects and offer help to those you feel need it. While your ambitious go-getting nature is admirable, if you don't allow yourself a much-needed break, you can push yourself to complete projects and can easily overwork yourself. You have a hard time saying no. You already have high standards when it comes to those in your life, but when you're not acting from a grounded sense of self, those high standards become almost unreachable and can cause resentment across the board.

When you're not working on something that is able to improve some facet of your life, you think you're just wasting time. You want to succeed and come through as the hard worker that you are—integrity and being true to your word are integral to your foundation—but sometimes this is done at the risk of your health and mood. Understanding that you are multilayered and respecting that limitations are not flaws will be enormously freeing for you.

LIBRA

You understand people, Libra. You're endlessly curious and fascinated by people and are passionate about getting to know people from various walks of life. As the sign of the Scales, you like to weigh things before taking action. You're someone who considers all factors and is a fan of making a pros and cons list. As an air sign, you offer careful and critical thought to any and every topic. This is why you're often the peacemaker in your social circles. Your process is often drawn out as you seek to find a peaceful resolution or harmonious answer that will benefit all parties involved. When you're acting from your anxiety, your decision-making becomes as slow as molasses. You don't like to be wrong or to disappoint others. So, instead of owning up to what you really want, for fear of hurting or offending others, you dissolve into a puddle of powerlessness and consistently come into stalemates in life. Whether it's moving forward with a job, relationship, or anything that needs your self-approval, you can become frustrated with your place in life and feel as if you're not moving forward. It's key for you to remain optimistic and embrace the unknown as you seek the clarity and groundedness you need to make the best decisions for your life.

SCORPIO

You're naturally intuitive, Scorpio, with a passionate and ambitious nature that makes you a boss at life. As a water sign, your inherent empathy helps you understand people on a deep level. However, when you're not feeling balanced, you can teeter more toward the dark and analytical side. You'll turn off your intuitive nature and instead let anxiety run the show. You become obsessed with worst-case scenarios and tread in pessimistic waters to the point that you'll forget to turn on your inner knowingness. You can also overthink and ruminate on subjects so much that you ultimately don't move forward. You might believe you're considering all your options, but you're actually procrastinating to the point of paralysis. You shut down and won't share any thoughts or ideas because you don't trust outside input or advice or you feel too proud to ask. When it comes to soothing your suspicious mind, Scorpio, you need to build your trust muscle while giving yourself permission to take action in your life.

SAGITTARIUS

Your independent and audacious energy craves freedom and exciting experiences, which is why you try to create a life that offers you exactly that. Your ideal life is being an entrepreneur or a freelancer who makes your own hours and has the flexibility to travel whenever you want. Feeling trapped ramps up your anxiety like a mofo. As a fire sign, you're headstrong in what you believe, and quick with the feisty verbiage. When you're fired up, you'll go toe-to-toe with someone in any type of debate or conflict, but sometimes your bark is bigger than your bite. If you don't feel confident, procrastination will kick in, and you won't finish what you started, emphasizing your worst fear: that you won't amount to anything great. When it comes to soothing your mind, Sag, it will help to find a sense of balance that keeps you grounded but also allows you to reach for the stars.

CAPRICORN

You're super ambitious and determined, and you hate to leave anything to chance. You know you can rely on yourself, but you have trouble trusting others to support you or even take on part of a plan that you've cautiously and carefully laid out. While you have big plans for your life, you're not much of a risk-taker. You prefer to take calculated actions under the false presumption that nothing can rock the boat if you've navigated it on the safest path. Your hustle can easily lead to burnout and frustration, especially if you don't think you're as far ahead as you think you should be. Little do you realize just how incredible you are. When it comes to soothing your critical mind, Capricorn, you need to self-regulate bursts of anxiety and frustration with grounding tools to help you realize you're imperfectly perfect.

AQUARIUS

You are a curious, free spirit who thrives on change and making change, Aquarius. On the other hand, you're a logical intellectual who's in search of continuous mental stimulation. Teetering more on one side than the other finds you imbalanced. Too rebellious and you become scattered and flighty; you won't finish anything or sit still. On the other side, as an air sign, you tend to overintellectualize everything and can become stuck. You can overanalyze so much that you feel frustrated or cause a situation to flatline—and you can also annoy others in the process. If you don't take the time to balance these two sides of your personality in a healthy way, you may find yourself oscillating between two very different extremes without any sure footing and not being able to find any sort of resolution or direction. When it comes to soothing your disparate mind, Aquarius, it's essential for you to ground yourself in the present for an equal amount of focus and freedom.

PISCES

You are a born creator, Pisces, and failing to appreciate or indulge that side of you leads you to feeling stuck and disenchanted with your life. Tapping into your creative side gives you a much-needed outlet for your feelings and ideas, which will only feed into other areas of your life. Honoring the dreamer within is important, but you must realize that your visions matter most when you're able to shape them into being. You add stress to your life when you fail to meld the poet with the practical. As a water sign, you feel much more comfortable leading with your feelings and imagining scenarios you wish to experience rather than actually doing them. While there's nothing wrong with visualizing your goals, taking action is the only way those goals can come to fruition. When it comes to soothing your distracted and worried mind, Pisces, it's helpful for you to remain in the moment as you explore and tap into your creative self.

MINDFUL MOMENTS FOR ALL ZODIAC SIGNS

---

*Journal Prompts to Understand
Your Messy Mind*

What do you love about your life?

What's the best part of your day?

What makes you feel overwhelmed?
What in your life stresses you out the most?

When you're feeling stressed or anxious, what are your typical coping mechanisms? How are these helpful? How are they not?

_____

_____

_____

_____

_____

_____

_____

_____

_____

_____

_____

_____

_____

_____

_____

_____

_____

_____

_____

What will bring more Zen into your life?

What activities bring you a sense of calm and peace?

What activity do you typically procrastinate?
Why do you put that off?

Which tasks do you look forward to completing and why?

When something doesn't go your way, how do you typically respond?

Do you learn from your mistakes? What are the biggest lessons you've learned from your past mistakes?

What are your top five achievements?
What about these achievements are you most proud of?

What are your top five goals right now?

Why are those goals so important to you?

What are your strengths?
How do they make you feel about yourself?

What are your weaknesses? How do they make you feel about yourself? Are you accepting of your weaknesses?

_____

_____

_____

_____

_____

_____

_____

_____

_____

_____

_____

_____

_____

_____

_____

_____

_____

_____

_____

_____

What was the best compliment you've ever received?

How did it make you feel? Do you agree with it?

_____

_____

_____

_____

_____

_____

_____

_____

_____

_____

_____

_____

_____

_____

_____

_____

_____

_____

Write a letter to your future self on a bad day.

What would you say to your future self to feel better?

_____

_____

_____

_____

_____

_____

_____

_____

_____

_____

_____

_____

_____

_____

_____

_____

_____

_____

_____

_____

Where in your schedule can you add
more mindful moments?

JOYFUL ACTIVITIES FOR YOUR MIND

Implement a morning routine. Morning routines are known to reduce stress and can include different things for everyone, from setting your schedule to enjoying a quiet moment alone with your coffee. Regardless of what it entails, it can help you start the day on a productive and positive note.

Start a creative hobby. Making the time for creativity can alleviate stress by connecting you to your inner child. Playtime is fun, remember?! So, paint. Dance. Put things together. Tear things apart. Do something that is constructive and helps you express yourself while channeling your energy and boosting your confidence.

Start a humblebrag file. When you're having a down day, it's important to remember your strengths and talents to shake off imposter syndrome and to remember the badass you are. Keep a humblebrag file on hand—in a Word doc, in your phone—that lists all your accomplishments and achievements as a quick reference.

Think of what could go right. Overthinkers often think of worst-case scenarios, which just causes you to stay stuck in your head. When you begin to overthink a situation, stop. Instead, visualize what could go right and keep referring to those thoughts.

Practice creative visualization meditation. Meditation helps to regulate the body's stress response to anxiety. Creative visualization is a good example of how to use your imagination to help you create whatever you want to happen in your life. Adding a creative visualization to your meditation practice can help you move closer to your goals by boosting your confidence.

Allow yourself to be a hot mess. Break out of your perfectionism by letting yourself be messy. Maybe it's not doing the dishes one night or not organizing your desk. It could even mean wearing sweats over a suit or not completing your weekly to-do list. Whatever it is, let yourself mess it up and be okay with it. Because it *is* okay.

Start a gratitude journal. Keeping a gratitude journal is a great way to keep yourself grounded and focused on what you have rather than what you don't have. The practice can lower stress, improve your sleep, and help you see how amazing you have it right now.

Stay accountable. Accountability is a great tool to help you bring your dreams into reality. Share your goals with friends and family and let them help you set deadlines and reminders to yourself. Motivate each other and take steps forward together each week.

Breathe and affirm your mantra. When life gets overwhelming, take the time to breathe mindfully—slowly count to three as you inhale and as you exhale—and repeat the mantras on the facing page to center yourself and return to calm.

Schedule downtime. Commit to creating an hour of downtime that allows you to focus on something less strenuous and more serene. Whether it's reading a fluffy novel or zoning out on Netflix, allow yourself to think about nothing important—just something nice and easy.

AFFIRMATIONS FOR MENTAL TLC

It's a good idea to get into the habit of repeating positive affirmations whenever you start beating yourself up for feeling less than. Stick them on your bathroom mirror or type them up on your phone. Recite them daily.

Fire signs (Aries, Leo, Sagittarius)
"When I allow myself to slow down, I can be my badass self."
"Rest is productive, too."
"My worth is determined by who I am, and not by what I do."

Earth signs (Taurus, Virgo, Capricorn)
"I am always supported by life, no matter what."
"I am perfectly imperfect."
"I don't need to sweat the small stuff."

Air signs (Gemini, Libra, Aquarius)
"I am centered and grounded."
"I believe in who I am and the decisions I make."
"It is easy for me to focus and concentrate."

Water signs (Cancer, Scorpio, Pisces)
"I am safe no matter what is happening around me."
"Every action I take moves me closer to my dreams."
"I have faith in myself and my abilities."

BODY

NOURISHING YOUR
ACTIVE BODY

~~~~~~~~~~

Neglecting R&R? Having trouble squeezing in
a sweat session? Here's how your sign reacts when you're
not properly nourishing your gorgeous body.

ARIES

As a fire sign, Aries, you're an adrenaline junkie, which is why it serves you to regularly engage in vigorous physical activities. When you don't have a physical outlet for your intense energy, you're more likely to become irritable. You might find yourself becoming short-tempered with your family or notice that you can't concentrate on your work because you long for a physical release. After all, your sign is ruled by Mars, the planet of action and aggression—moving your body helps you tap into your innate power and satisfies your competitive side. For you, sweat = success. On the flip side, you tend to overdo it physically, too. Don't forget that your fierce spirit also requires soothing, and your body definitely deserves a break from such intense movement. When it comes to taking care of your body, Aries, find balance between an equal share of challenging, competitive activities and calming, grounding ones.

TAURUS

Let's be real, Taurus. Physical activity isn't at the top of your to-do list. In fact, it's probably near the bottom. The trick, then, is to find the exercises that speak to your slow-and-steady soul. As an earth sign, it serves you to stick to activities that are grounding and nourishing, as well as those that require your senses to be totally engaged. Because you're ruled by Venus, the planet of beauty and grace, you're more likely to enjoy physical activities that make you feel and look graceful, like Barre and Pilates. This way you'll not only be working out your body and mind, you'll also be developing confidence and learning to love and appreciate yourself. When it comes to nourishing your body, Taurus, finding balance between what feels comfortable and challenging is key to upping your game so that you can remain healthy and happy.

GEMINI

Getting you to commit to a regular workout routine is like pulling teeth. You prefer to live life spontaneously and need a lot of variety to keep from being bored. When it comes to how you prefer to spend your downtime, as an air sign, you veer toward intellectual pursuits rather than physical exercise. You also tend to eat a lot of takeout and processed food simply because it's quick and easy and doesn't require a lot of thought or preparation. However, taking the time to nourish your body and finding a physical outlet for your hyperactivity can balance your bouncy energy and improve your focus while also enhancing your health and physical well-being. Your chaotic energy needs a self-care routine that offers both stability and a lot of variety to keep you interested and engaged for the long haul. You need to feel that you're constantly being mentally stimulated in order to endure the sweaty mess that lies ahead.

CANCER

You're the homebody of the zodiac—you love being at home more than being anywhere else in the world and find it challenging to leave the house for anything, let alone working out. As a water sign, you prefer to flow. Overly regimented programs don't work with your natural yearning for flexibility and fluidity. You're also someone who needs to follow your intuition. Doing the next big trend isn't going to help you stick to a routine. You need to do something that feels right to you and works for your lifestyle, but that also ignites the fire within. The downside of not exercising means you could pull farther into your shell and isolate yourself even more. When it comes to nourishing your body, Cancer, you can help keep your body healthy by connecting to a consistent routine that keeps you connected to yourself.

LEO

You love to be the best and look your best, Leo, so sticking to an exercise regimen is typically easy for you. As a fire sign, you're driven to succeed with unwavering passion and enthusiasm, which makes physical exercise a fantastic release for your high energy and something that you actually look forward to. You're always on the lookout for a new challenge or a physical activity that stretches your limits and builds your confidence. When you're feeling imbalanced, you let your ego run the show. Insecurities can get the best of you. In order to remain healthy and happy when it comes to nourishing your body, Leo, stay in your creative flow with exercise. Balance your obsession with looking and being the best by concentrating on what you love about your body. Explore enjoyable activities that connect you with others and your best, fun-loving self.

VIRGO

You're obsessed with everything self-care. You understand that the most important work you can do in life is the work you do on yourself, which is why you're the first to try the latest fitness and wellness trends whether that's trying out the latest green smoothie or attending (literally) the hottest yoga class. As an air sign ruled by Mercury, you want your body to be as sharp and on-point as your mind. You can become very frustrated with yourself if you're not progressing as well as you would like. On the opposite end of the spectrum, you're often so busy that you don't take the time to relax or exercise. When it comes to self-care for your body, Virgo, it's important to understand that not everything has to be a project, and especially not your body. Less pushing, more flowing.

LIBRA

You like to look groomed and polished, Libra, and you love feeling yourself. Aesthetics are everything to you, so when it comes to fitness and wellness, you'll put the time in to ensure that your body fits the image that you think looks most pleasing. As an air sign, though, you're not super pumped about getting pumped anyway. You'd rather spend your spare time learning new things and gaining knowledge. Couple that with your inner social butterfly, and your schedule is often too full of activities and engagements to focus on nourishing your body. Because you thrive in social environments, focus on enjoying yourself and connecting with your body in fun ways that aren't just about looking good, but feeling good, too. Balance your flighty and chatty temperament with an equal share of social activities and calming, grounding ones.

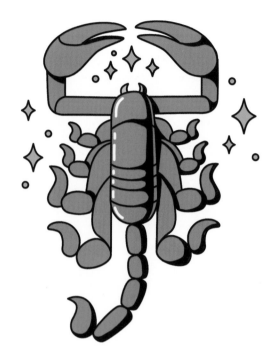

SCORPIO

You're intense, Scorpio, so when you don't create time for physical activity in your life, you may feel overwhelmed. As a water sign, if you're imbalanced, your feelings tend to overwhelm and flood you, so being in your body is good for you. Ruled by Mars, the planet of action and aggression, your passionate side longs to express itself physically. With Pluto, the planet of transformation and rebirth, as your other ruler, you're more likely to stick to physical activities that allow you to expand spiritually. For you, Scorpio, seeing exercise as a way to tap into a more expansive side of yourself will help you keep evolving as the badass sexy soul you are.

SAGITTARIUS

As a fire sign, you're innately someone who thrives on being on the go. Sitting still isn't an option for you. Couple that with your adventurous energy, and working out your intensity is a must. However, like most people, life can get in the way of going to the gym. You might be traveling so much that it's almost impossible to squeeze in a workout. Physical activity is integral to who you are, but because your ruling planet is Jupiter, the planet of expansion and higher learning, it's also important that you seek out activities that challenge you and ask you to grow. You'll try anything once—including death-defying feats. There's nothing wrong with pushing yourself, but not if you're modeling Evel Knievel. It's crucial to balance your need to challenge yourself with keeping yourself safe and to realize that while you disdain rest days, they won't kill you (unlike extreme sports).

CAPRICORN

You're someone who likes to keep moving, Capricorn, because it gives you a sense of purpose. Sitting still makes you feel lazy, and you hate feeling lazy. You see life as filled with possibilities and things to do—why would anyone waste a moment by not doing anything? Without a healthy workout routine, you're prone to overworking yourself and never looking up from your work or latest project. Thanks to your earth element, you have a grounded gravitas to you. But if you're caught up in the rat race, you forget that side of you. Going outdoors and taking the time to be active in nature is the perfect solution to keeping your physical self-care in check. When it comes to taking care of your body, Cap, balance your workaholic tendencies with an equal share of competitive activities and grounding and balancing ones that still make you feel accomplished.

AQUARIUS

Creating time for physical activity isn't at the top of your priority list. As an air sign, you're so busy living in your head—thinking about and analyzing your latest work project, strategizing a new plan of action, or simply reading a book or studying—that you don't think about your body. In fact, you can become so engrossed in whatever you're doing that you might not even remember the last time you ate. If you're to engage in any sort of physical self-care, it needs to be quirky, varied, and something that engages both your mind and body. And if it connects to technology or is linked to the latest fad, your interest is definitely piqued. Since you're a sponge of knowledge and information, reading up on fitness and personal training, and understanding and learning about the body, could also be great ways for you to stay motivated.

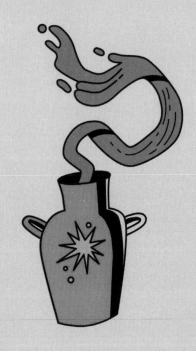

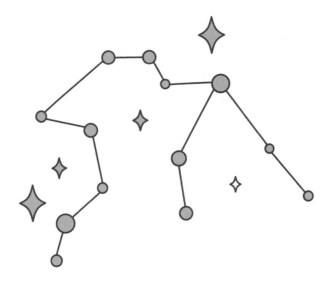

PISCES

You already feel a little floaty and dreamy on the regular, Pisces, but when you don't take time to nourish your body, you're bound to feel disconnected. You would easily skip out on the gym to stay home underneath the covers, listening to sad songs and being flooded with feelings without knowing how or what to do in order to feel better. As a water sign, you're built to put emotions first. You'd rather flow or be still than sweat and move. However, it's important to remember that exercise isn't just an effective way to stay healthy; it's also an awesome grounding tool that returns you to your body and the present moment. You're easily distracted, and you have trouble making decisions, especially when you're not feeling good about yourself. When it comes to taking care of your body, Pisces, balance your smooshy emotions with activities that ground you and tune into the best parts of you: creative and flowy.

NOURISHING MOMENTS FOR ALL ZODIAC SIGNS

Journal Prompts to Give Yourself Some Body Love

Describe your relationship with your body.

What does your body mean to you?

_____

_____

_____

_____

_____

_____

_____

_____

_____

_____

_____

_____

_____

_____

_____

_____

_____

_____

_____

_____

_____

What do you love and appreciate about your body? Why?

What are things that you don't like about your body? Why?

How could you be more gentle and kind to your body?

What are your favorite ways to move your body?

What are some instances when you've been
especially proud of your body?

_____

_____

_____

_____

_____

_____

_____

_____

_____

_____

_____

_____

_____

_____

_____

_____

_____

_____

_____

Do you like to cook? Why or why not? If so, what is your favorite dish to cook? If you're a novice cook, what would you like to try to create in the kitchen?

What is your favorite food? What makes it so delicious?

What are some of your favorite ways to relax your body?

_____

_____

_____

_____

_____

_____

_____

_____

_____

_____

_____

_____

_____

_____

_____

_____

_____

_____

What are some physical activities you would like to try?

What does "nourishing" your body look and feel like to you?

How can you implement more body self-care

into your daily routine?

JOYFUL ACTIVITIES TO TREAT YOUR BODY

Get outside. Getting outdoors often is essential for our well-being. Walking, biking, hiking, and running outside are all perfect examples of workouts that don't feel like exercise because you're too busy enjoying yourself and the fresh air. Exercising outdoors will help you feel grounded and connected to your best self (while also getting in that much-needed cardio boost).

Cook something new and healthy. Challenging your kitchen skills and committing to cooking something new and healthy each week is a terrific way to nourish your body. People who eat more home-cooked meals regularly tend to be happier and healthier with higher energy levels—plus, it'll feel great to accomplish something new each week.

Implement meal planning and prep. Resolving to eat more nutritious foods takes a great deal of willpower, but implementing a meal plan can help you stay on the right track. While meal planning may seem monotonous at first, treat it as a creative challenge by mixing up your meals each week.

Commit to home workouts. Bring the workout to you. There are a variety of online workout platforms to keep you interested and that offer you the opportunity to do a workout that feels good to you on that particular day. You'll continually challenge your body while never having to leave the comfort of home.

Start a gratitude list about your body. List everything you love about your body and what your body has done for you on a daily basis.

Give your body props. Admire your body in the mirror and say aloud what you love about yourself. Recite body-positive mantras and affirmations like, "I love and accept my body today," "My body deserves respect and kindness," and "I enjoy nourishing my body every day."

Try a new physical activity. Seek out new ways to move your body that challenge you and get your creative juices flowing. From trying out a new dance class to signing up for a marathon or exploring a new hiking trail, everything and anything goes.

Allow yourself a cheat day. A healthy lifestyle requires balance. Whether it's taking a day off from hitting the gym or allowing yourself to splurge on some cheese fries, allow yourself to feel no guilt. Give yourself a break and do something fun. Everything in moderation, right?

Rest and relax your body. Your body needs a rest. Whether that's allowing yourself some extra Zs, booking a massage, or relaxing in a bubble bath, taking some time out to rest your bod is a great way to de-stress.

Partner up. Hiring a personal trainer or finding an accountability buddy are effective methods to keep you motivated and help you stick to your workout routine. Plus, it'll give you a workout buddy, which makes exercise more fun.

LOVE-YOUR-BODY RITUALS

Fire signs (Aries, Leo, Sagittarius): You are the passionate trailblazers of the zodiac. You're highly competitive and passionate about winning, so signing up for competitive races like the Ironman or joining a local sports league will give you the exercise you need while also satisfying your desire to compete. A rest day is key for someone like you who constantly pushes and challenges yourself physically—not to mention someone who is always on the move.

Earth signs (Taurus, Virgo, Capricorn): You are the steady and practical members of the zodiac. You come into your element when you connect with nature. Physical outdoor activities like mountain climbing, hiking, and trail running are great exercises that are challenging enough for you while also grounding your energy. You're also the loners of the zodiac, so try solo activities, like paddle boarding, golf, and snowboarding or skiing.

Air signs (Gemini, Libra, Aquarius): You are the thinkers of the zodiac. Mind-body exercises like martial arts or yoga are excellent choices for you. Regular yoga practice creates mental clarity and calmness; increases body awareness; relieves chronic stress; relaxes the mind; centers attention; and sharpens concentration. You also like the company of others, so joining a fitness class or exercising with a buddy is a great choice for you.

Water signs (Cancer, Scorpio, Pisces): You are the water babies of the zodiac. Taking part in non-competitive water sports, whether it's swimming or water aerobics, is a great way to move your body that feels comfortable to you and makes you feel confident. Also, relaxing in a warm bath helps to relieve stress and emotional overload. Add a little lavender essential oil to help calm your nerves, and visualize your intense feelings dissolving into the tub.

SOUL

TAPPING INTO YOUR SPIRITUAL SIDE

~~~~~~~~

Are you having trouble connecting to
the deeper, more soulful side of life?
Here's how you respond when you're feeling out
of touch with your true spirit.

ARIES

Sometimes you're just too busy achieving the next goal to focus on what it means to be a soul. As a fire sign, you think you ought to be doing something more productive with your time than pondering the meaning of life. This is why you tend to view spirituality as something less esoteric and more practical. When you're living life from the truth of who you are, others see you as a guiding light and, as a result, start taking action toward fulfilling their own dreams and goals. You invite others to tune into their own courage and lightness by embodying the same, and that's how you find your sacredness. An Aries's spirit needs to feel purposeful. Create the time to slow down and calm your blazing energy so you can feel connected to the truth of who you are.

TAURUS

Your true nature, Taurus, is someone who's deeply connected to the world and those around you. As an earth sign, you have a great appreciation for nature, and people adore being in your soothing and generous presence, thanks to your ruling planet, Venus. Connecting to your soul means allowing yourself to see how truly lovable you are without attaching love to a designer label or any other thing, and it means remembering that your oneness begins with being in nature. Seeking internal pleasure and safety is your path to coming home to your true self and to a world beyond the physical. When you recognize that what makes you feel whole and safe is actually *you*, Taurus, you can finally let go and be free. In order to connect to your soul, Taurus, you need to feel at ease and at peace while experiencing the things that are most enjoyable to the Bull.

GEMINI

As an air sign, Gemini, you're naturally drawn to questioning the world around you. Your inherent thirst for knowledge has probably led you to explore different topics and philosophies on religion and spirituality. Diving deep into your soul, however, requires lots of solo time, focus, and the implementation of a spiritual ritual of some kind, which can be a bit difficult for you to commit to. As someone who has trouble being in the moment and concentrating on one thing at a time, it takes work for you to be still and listen to your inner voice. However, the work of spirit is ever constant and ever evolving, and doing things we aren't comfortable with is, ultimately, the work of the soul. In order for you to feel connected to your soul, you need to slow your busy mind and drop down into the truth of who you are, distraction-free.

CANCER

As a water sign and the maternal figure of the zodiac, Cancer, you're naturally compassionate and nurturing. Empathy involves identifying with others and recognizing our common humanity, and it is a powerful bridge. However, sometimes your intense feelings become too much for you to bear, and you retreat into your shell. It may be easy for you to dismiss just how powerful your open heart can be. You might think you're not doing or being enough for your community. Allow yourself to see the suffering in the world and know that simply showing up as your true self is more than enough to help heal the world and experience heaven on earth. You, Cancer, need to celebrate your innate intuition while also showing up for others in your community to help you connect to a world outside of yourself.

LEO

You're so concerned with looking for external excitement and approval rather than seeking fulfillment internally, Leo, that you have trouble fitting in soulful inventory into your busy social calendar. As a fire sign, you love exciting projects and experiencing life in big and beautiful ways rather than sitting still and going within. What you fail to realize is that your innate gifts—confidence, self-expression, and your big heart—can help you connect to your soul. When you begin to see that inner exploration is just as valid as (if not more valid than) outer exploration and that people love you for who you truly are, you'll see the light that you've possessed all along. For your spirit to grow and evolve, Leo, it's important to implement regular selfless practices to further connect you with the world around you and remind yourself just how kind and loving you really are.

VIRGO

Spirituality is part of who you are, Virgo—you are meant to live from your soul.
As an earth sign, you are intricately connected to the world around you. It's easy for
you to feel at peace in nature and see the universe as an expansion of love that
encompasses us all. However, you can't help but be a perfectionist, so you have a
hard time allowing life to be spontaneous and magical. You seek to control the
outcomes of life rather than letting them unfold. It will help you to find a spiritual
practice that's grounding and flexible. It's also important for you to spend time alone
for personal reflection—and to do this when you're not seeking to fix yourself but to
just be with yourself. Perhaps the biggest piece of your soulful self-care is letting
go of perfection and control, Virgo, and knowing you're enough as you are.
Allow life, and others, to show up for you.

LIBRA

You can be so busy with your packed schedule that you have little time to think about your soul's purpose, which is ironic because you have one of the most loving souls on the planet. You care about people, and you believe in the goodness of the human race. However, you're more likely to seek oneness from the approval of your friends and family rather than going within. As an air sign, it's easy for you to get in your head about others' approval. You need to trust that you are lovable, Libra, just as you are—no strings attached. Your ability to bring people together and make them feel good is a blessing; but the messaging only gets through when your love comes from a clear channel. You're doing your soul's work when you realize that you have nothing to prove and that you possess all the tools, knowledge, and love you need from within. Be still and listen.

SCORPIO

You have a clear sense of how you think the universe and soul work on a very philosophical and deep level. But sometimes you have a hard time when it comes to putting your work into practice. This happens when you're connecting to spirit from your mind rather than your soul, which stems from a deep-rooted distrust of yourself. You wonder if your beliefs indeed stack up, and you're scared to be disappointed. If you let your constant questioning get the better of you, it can cause you to second-guess the world and all that you know to be true. But that's the ultimate test of faith. It's leaping before the net appears. Walk the spiritual path and you'll soon see others following you.

SAGITTARIUS

You feel most connected to your spirit when you're leading a cause or spearheading a project that connects you to your passions: expansion and humanity. Ruled by Jupiter, the planet of growth and expansion, it's natural for you to seek a higher consciousness for yourself and the world around you. And, as a fire sign, you want to be the one who leads the charge for that change. However, in your quest for knowledge, you also tend to be a lone wolf. You think you must disconnect from others as you try to sort out things on your own. But if you're to be someone who promotes the expansion of humanity, you need to accept the help of others sometimes and welcome them on your journey. By welcoming the company and goodwill of others, you will ultimately possess the confidence to be a source of wisdom and a true leader of change.

CAPRICORN

~~~~~~~~~~~~~~~~~~~~~~~

For someone as practical and skeptical as you, Capricorn, you're open to exploring spirituality—but on your terms. As symbolized by the Sea Goat, you're a mystic rooted in traditionalism. As an earth element, you're also a practical thinker who prefers their feet on the ground. Your dual nature can cause some discomfort and dissonance in your life when you don't take the time to regularly check into your spirit. When you lead with practicality, you'll seek fulfillment from external achievements rather than inner fulfillment. There's something special and otherworldly about you, Cap. You create your own reality alongside an inner knowingness that you're destined for more, and this knowingness stems from a belief that extends beyond the logical. When you stop leading with your mind and instead surrender to your soul, you access a divine path leading to where you're meant to be.

AQUARIUS

~~~~~~~~~~~~~~~~~~~~~~~

You are a visionary, Aquarius, so you're typically very clear on what you want to accomplish and how you want to do it. As an air sign, you're intellectualizing and brainstorming nonstop. However, you can become so headstrong about what you want to pursue that no matter how earnest and true your intentions might be, your push for progress can develop into a battle of right versus wrong ("right" being your opinion and "wrong" being anyone's opinion that isn't yours). The beauty of your mind, Aquarius, is how forward-thinking it is and how much you believe in the power of transformation and change. While your individualism and intelligence give you a unique life perspective that can promote a revolution, leaning into the community will fill your cup and deliver results more than you know. Cohesion and inclusion are how you reach true consciousness.

PISCES

You are the most spiritual sign of the zodiac, Pisces. You are ruled by Neptune, the planet of dreams, inspiration, and spirituality. Connecting to your soul is your natural sixth sense. You are the spiritual guru of your tribe and will gladly ponder life's meaning and your connection to it all the livelong day. You believe we're on earth for a reason and that it's your life's work to figure it out. As a water sign, you would rather indulge in your visions and undergo intense spiritual experiences than, say, do something more grounded, like taking a walk in the park with a friend or helping at a soup kitchen or animal shelter. Spreading your compassionate, big heart and helpfulness to others, you show how powerful the intentions and actions of one person can be.

SPIRITUAL MOMENTS FOR ALL ZODIAC SIGNS

*Journal Prompts
to Explore Your Soul*

What does spirituality mean to you?

Do you believe you have a soul? Why or why not?

What are some activities that lift your spirit?

Describe some instances in your life when you've experienced
a "miracle" or a "synchronistic event." How did they make you feel?
Did they make you believe in serendipity?
Why or why not?

_____

_____

_____

_____

_____

_____

_____

_____

_____

_____

_____

_____

_____

_____

_____

_____

_____

_____

What are you most grateful for in your life right now?

What gives you a sense of purpose?

What does community mean to you? Do you have a community?
How does being a part of that community make you
feel about others and your place in the world?

What do you think makes the world a better place?
How would you like to contribute to that?

List **10** inherent gifts that you have to offer to your community and the world.

1. _____

2. _____

3. _____

4. _____

5. _____

6. _____

7. _____

8. _____

9. _____

10. _____

What are your guiding values in life?

When have you felt most connected to your spirituality
and/or a force that couldn't be explained?

How and where can you implement more
soulful activities in your life?

ACTIVITIES TO HELP
LIFT YOUR SPIRIT

Make alone time a regular thing. Making the time to be alone is a precious gift that you can give yourself. It allows you to recharge and tune into yourself, free of distraction and other people's energy. This could include anything from going for a walk in a park to quietly reading a book alone. Just make sure whatever you're doing requires some solo stillness.

Practice mindfulness during the day. Mindfulness is simply slowing down and observing the physical and emotional sensations you are experiencing in the moment—this could be anything from taking a walk to eating your food. Continuously practicing mindfulness throughout your day, whether you're on the bus or at your desk, can help you stay connected to the world around you.

Do small, kind things often. Whether it's treating a stranger to a coffee or buying groceries for an elderly neighbor, small acts of service connect you to your natural loving soul and remind you that generosity is how we honor and express human value and our interconnectedness to each other.

Meditate. A daily meditation practice will help you surrender to the present moment, connect with your authentic soul in total solitude, and release any fears that keep you clinging to what no longer serves you.

Establish a spiritual practice. Developing a ritual around your spiritual practice creates consistency and sacredness. By dedicating time to a practice that feels right to you—whether that's meditation, praying, or lighting a candle and writing in your journal—you can regularly excavate your soul, which will keep you feeling connected and at peace.

Volunteer with a charity or organization. Volunteering with a charity will fulfill your soul while helping you do some good in the world.

Dive deep into spiritual texts. Reading and educating yourself about different perspectives and history is a great way to understand different tenets of religion and spirituality. It also helps you get a sense of how to construct a belief system that works for you.

Sit outside in nature and observe. Just being with yourself, quieting your mind, and observing the world around you are some of the most powerful and spiritual experiences you can have. The practice will help you observe that we live in an abundant and beautiful universe.

Connect with your spirit through writing. Free writing is a powerful way to connect with your inner voice and spirit. Take a quiet moment for yourself and allow yourself to write from a very still place. In this way, you are connecting to your inner guide, who knows you best. You'll feel guided and protected.

SOULFUL RITUALS

Fire signs (Aries, Leo, Sagittarius): Try a burn ritual. A burning ritual is an ancient tradition that's performed to let go of things that no longer serve you. This can be done on specific, powerful days that mark new beginnings—like New Year's Day or your birthday, for example—or anytime when you feel that you need to let go of negativity in your life, like after a relationship ends. A burn ritual can be whatever you'd like it to be, but typically includes writing down what you would like to burn, setting a positive intention on what you would like to call into your life, and lighting your paper on fire in a fireproof bowl within a safe space.

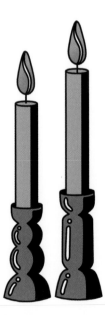

Earth signs (Taurus, Virgo, Capricorn): See the sacred outdoors. You inherently find nature healing. As an earth sign, being outdoors naturally grounds you and helps put life in perspective for you. Regularly removing yourself from the hustle and bustle of our modern-day consumer culture and getting into the great outdoors will help you discover your own true nature and connect to a deep level of peace and clarity. Taking time to connect with the soothing rhythm of Mother Nature is a great way for you to tune into your spirit.

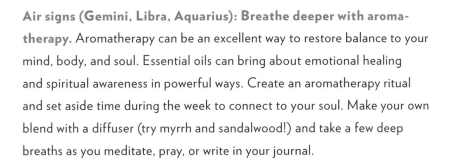

Air signs (Gemini, Libra, Aquarius): Breathe deeper with aromatherapy. Aromatherapy can be an excellent way to restore balance to your mind, body, and soul. Essential oils can bring about emotional healing and spiritual awareness in powerful ways. Create an aromatherapy ritual and set aside time during the week to connect to your soul. Make your own blend with a diffuser (try myrrh and sandalwood!) and take a few deep breaths as you meditate, pray, or write in your journal.

Water signs (Cancer, Scorpio, Pisces): Commit to a lunar practice. As water signs, you might find yourself more affected by the lunar cycle (since the moon does influence the tides). For example, during a full or new moon you might find yourself deeper in your feelings than usual. Take advantage of these powerful days to tune into the potent spiritual energies. Meditate, set an intention for the week, and create some moon water (simply leave a glass or container of water outdoors to charge under the moonlight) to further develop your intuition and connection to the universe.

MOOD

EMBRACING
YOUR EMOTIONS

Identifying your emotional triggers will
help you understand—and better control—
your moods and phases.

ARIES

Expressing emotions doesn't come easily to you, Aries. You like to feel in control and that you can handle everything and anything. More importantly, you're committed to doing everything by yourself. While you do feel happiest when you're running the show, sometimes your militant approach to tasks, work, and even relationships masks your immense vulnerability. The truth is, you feel a lot, Aries, but you resist opening up to others for fear of showing weakness. You long for community, but you don't trust that others will include you in their plans, so you take it upon yourself to make things happen. Your biggest lesson when it comes to coping with emotional self-care is realizing that you don't have to go it alone. When you share your innermost feelings with a loved one, you'll begin to discover that you're accepted for being you no matter what.

TAURUS

Your ruling planet, Venus, instills within you the gift of connection, which is why you're so awesome at creating and cultivating lifelong friendships and relationships. Sweet-natured and compassionate, you will go the extra mile for those you care about, and your inner circle appreciates that about you. When you're not feeling balanced, it's easy for you to become hurt over simple mishaps, like an ignored text. Your anxiety is likely to skyrocket, and your mind will spin with worry over what you've done wrong. As an earth element, you pride yourself on your loyalty and attention to detail, so you're tough on yourself when you receive the slightest criticism from a loved one. On the outside, you're a pillar of strength with a stiff upper lip; but on the inside, you're as creamy as an Oreo center. When it comes to your emotional self-care, Taurus, it would help you to understand that you're valuable just as you are. You're a gifted creator and friend, and your presence and know-how are welcomed and admired.

GEMINI

When it comes to emotions, Gemini, you hide your feelings underneath a mask of good humor and offer sarcastic comments in lieu of vulnerable advice. Emotions can make you feel uncomfortable. This can cause you to come across as unsympathetic and unfeeling. However, nothing could be further from the truth. Behind your jokes and bravado lies a deep-feeling soul. You're so busy keeping everyone happy and enter-tained, but you secretly long to be taken care of and truly seen for all of you. As an air sign, though, vulnerability doesn't come easily to you, as you tend to rationalize and compartmentalize feelings. But you're human, Gemini. As much as you try to justify that logic outweighs emotions, you can't help but feel what you feel. Learning to not only accept and embrace those feelings, Gemini, but to express them softly is how you first tend to your emotional self-care.

CANCER

You're a kind, loving, and welcoming soul, Cancer. You're quick to take care of loved ones and their needs before yourself, so you often forget to fill up your own tank first. When you're not tending to your emotional self-care, you can also be clingy and posses- sive of your friends. Your insecurity can override your sense of self, and eventually can cause you to feel unbalanced and confused as to who you are and what you need to feel happy and healthy. Thanks to your double whammy of emotions, courtesy of the water element and the moon that rules your sign, you are already someone who lives and breathes complex emotions. When it comes to your emotional self-care, Cancer, you must nurture yourself the same way that you nurture others. It's important for you to stand on your own two feet and claim sovereignty over your emotions.

LEO

Your emotions are huge. You definitely wear the crown of Drama Queen or King when you're not feeling balanced. When you're upset or in a bad mood, everyone knows it. Even if a friend calls and needs your support and advice, you'll twist the conversation back to you so that you're the one who's receiving the TLC. You can also get caught up in a cycle of constant social comparison to others, seeking approval through "likes" and other external accolades to feel validated. When you're acting like this, it's easy—and accurate—for people to accuse you of being self-centered. What you're actually craving, though, is love and understanding. When it comes to emotional self-care, Leo, one of your biggest lessons is learning how to facilitate confidence and self-love from within. When you learn how to better balance your emotions, you'll also be a better friend— which, thanks to your big heart, is what you're genuinely good at.

VIRGO

In low times, as a naturally independent person, Virgo, you need your space. However, this can be to your detriment, as you tend to shut out people and convince yourself that you don't need anyone. As an earth element, you think problems can be solved with your intellect and mind. You choose to be stoic rather than soft. One of your biggest lessons in emotional self-care is learning to honor your emotions. If you allow that to be a freeing experience for you, it will connect you to another part of yourself that you often ignore—your heart center. Emotions are to be experienced and expressed, too—it's what makes us human. When it comes to nurturing your emotions, Virgo, it's key to acknowledge that you have them in the first place. It's essential to create time and space to express and feel your feels.

LIBRA

~~~~~~~~~~~~~~~~~~~~~

While you're naturally loving, kind, and a popular person—thanks to the planet Venus—there is an aloofness about you, Libra. You flit from social group to social group, stacking your calendar with various activities so that you keep your social status intact while keeping the vibe light and fun. You know a lot of people—but do you really know them? And do they really know the real you? When you don't honor your emotional self-care, you intellectualize emotional interactions, and it's difficult for you to openly express your vulnerability. This explains why, as much as you desire a deeper connection with others, you fear exposing your underbelly. You don't trust that others will accept you, flaws and all. For you, committing to an emotional self-care routine means connecting to your true emotions while pouring on self-compassion and love to allow the real you to shine through.

SCORPIO

~~~~~~~~~~~~~~~~~~~~~

You feel a lot of emotions, Scorpio. As a water sign, being in your feels is second nature for you. You have a lot of feelings that often oscillate throughout the day—you can be as moody as a mood ring—and when you're not grounded, they can overrun your day, confusing not only yourself but those around you. You're terrified of being hurt or judged for your shadow; if anyone is cognizant of their shadow in the zodiac, it's you, Scorpio. You know that everyone has a good side and bad side to them—this is because of your other planetary ruler, Pluto—and when you're not nourishing your emotional self-care, you can focus too much on your flaws and faults. You might let shame overcome you, which prevents you from making connections with others. Your emotional self-care, Scorpio, relies on your ability to self-regulate your intense emotions while also allowing yourself to open up and see the lighter side of life.

SAGITTARIUS

On your best days, you have a happy-go-lucky, positive attitude that lifts spirits, Sagittarius. You have friends in many different social circles, which you love. However, sometimes your cavalier approach to relationships hides your fear of getting close to others. Your fierce independence can quickly morph into aloofness, and you're known to disappear on friends and family for periods of time to "do you." You struggle with being judged and accepted by others due to your unconventional lifestyle and views. You assume others won't "get you," so you would rather shut them out than face any criticism. It's a double-edged sword because by shutting out people before they can get close to you, you'll never know if they actually like and accept you for you—which they probably would. Relationships are a two-way street. You don't have to sacrifice your independence for the right connections, but there is some goodness and joy to be had when you see that life can be better with others. Compromise and cooperation can be gifts to you, too, if you let them.

CAPRICORN

You're often a serious and stoic Goat. You're so caught up in the busyness of your world and achieving your goals that it can be difficult for you to crack a smile. That's too bad because underneath that measured demeanor is someone who's adept with a wry and sarcastic comment. You're funny, Capricorn! But when you're bogged down by your tasks and errands, you forget that life's not that serious. Or at least it doesn't have to be all the time. Finding your balance between letting your hair down and being true to your need for space is the sweet spot when it comes to nurturing your emotions. When it comes to emotional self-care, you need to acknowledge and access all of your feelings, Capricorn, even the lighter ones. By doing so, you'll be able to balance your work with play and enjoy the ones you love the most, including yourself.

AQUARIUS

As friendly and altruistic as you are, Aquarius, you tend to come off as cold, indifferent, and aloof to even your closest friends. You're a loner by nature and like your space, but when you're not nurturing your emotions, you can be even more impersonal toward those around you. As an air sign, you're more disconnected from your feels, preferring to lead with logic and a sense of fair judgment. Emotions are messy and cause attachments, and you like to stay as detached and drama-free as possible. You tend to withdraw and ruminate when things get heavy, but sometimes laughter really is the best medicine—and you have a wicked sense of humor that your friends really enjoy. When it comes to your emotional self-care, allowing yourself to experience your feelings full-on and seeing the beauty of connection will help you feel holistically happy.

PISCES

Expressing emotions is second nature to you, Pisces. As an emotional and intuitive water sign, you're basically a walking and talking beating heart. You feel and absorb everything from everyone. You're an extreme empath, which makes it difficult for you to determine which feelings are yours and which belong to others. When you're not taking the time to nurture your emotional self-care, you're vulnerable to developing depression, anxiety, and emotional burnout. You can become so despondent that doing anything and going anywhere become almost impossible. When it comes to coping with emotional self-care, your biggest lesson is learning how to control your emotions and not the other way around. Your empathic nature is a beautiful gift, but only when you're able to learn to honor your abilities with confidence and self-love.

MOOD-SOOTHING MOMENTS FOR ALL ZODIAC SIGNS

Journal Prompts to Get Acquainted with Your Feels

How do you feel right now?

Is it easy for you to name your emotions?

What makes you happy?

_____

_____

_____

_____

_____

_____

_____

_____

_____

_____

_____

_____

_____

_____

_____

_____

_____

_____

_____

_____

_____

What do you fear the most?

When do you feel sad?

How do you react when you're angry?

Which instances are you most triggered by?

Are these instances tied to a particular memory?

If so, what feelings and behaviors have come from this memory?

How have they been helpful or not helpful to you?

_____

_____

_____

_____

_____

_____

_____

_____

_____

_____

_____

_____

_____

_____

_____

_____

_____

What does vulnerability mean to you?

How does it make you feel?

_____

_____

_____

_____

_____

_____

_____

_____

_____

_____

_____

_____

_____

_____

_____

_____

_____

_____

_____

_____

_____

Do you find it easy to express your emotions? Why or why not?
Do you like when others express their emotions to you?
Why or why not?

Which emotion(s) do you feel the most on a regular basis?

Which ones are harder for you to express?

What do you find most curious about that?

Where in your body do you experience emotional pain?

How does your body feel when you're feeling joyful?

What brings you the most peace?

CALMING AND CONNECTING ACTIVITIES TO HELP BALANCE YOUR MOOD

— ✦ —

Feeling upset? Text a friend. Opening up to a friend about what's bothering you and asking for their support—whether it's to help cheer you up or to ask them to take the reins for the next hangout—will take a load off your shoulders while deepening your bond.

Take a breath. When you're feeling triggered and wanting to lash out, focusing on your breathing will help regulate your nervous system. The benefits of breathwork are threefold: it immediately brings a sense of calm to your body, it helps your mind to focus and clear, and it helps you to refrain from acting impulsively, bringing awareness to the present moment and helping your intense emotions to subside.

Sit with your feelings. Vulnerability is the driving force of forming connections with others and with ourselves. Being able to reveal your feelings and desires to other people means recognizing that it's okay to feel big feelings. Don't be quick to dismiss or rationalize your feelings. Instead, sit with them and acknowledge them, and, most of all, allow yourself to feel what you're feeling without judgment. Dare to be uncomfortable, and see what growth and information are coming up for you. Then extend yourself a big dose of self-compassion for who you are.

Set boundaries. Learning to set boundaries is an effective way to protect your own energy, handle conflict effectively, and take charge of your emotions. Get clear on what you need to feel safe, and then name your limits on what is and isn't acceptable both for yourself and others.

Take a break from social media. Take regular daily breaks from social media to help cease FOMO and any trigger—for instance, not getting a like for your latest post—that makes you feel invalid or disapproved of. Consider taking regular social media detoxes by logging out for a week every month or so.

Watch something funny. Laughter sometimes is life's best medicine. Humor your funny bone and make time to watch a funny movie or TV show regularly. Even looking at funny memes or talking to a funny friend will do the trick. Welcome the light into your life to balance the dark.

Consider therapy. We all need some help sometimes, and seeing a therapist could be the best thing for you if you're struggling to cope with and/or process your emotions. Therapy is a great tool to help connect you with your emotions and obstacles. Whether it's in person on an app, therapy is major emotional TLC.

Come back to your body. When you're emotionally flooded or feeling extra sensitive, ground yourself in your body and into the present moment. Wiggling your toes and caressing your wrists slowly while actively relaxing any tension in your body with five big exhales will calm your sensory and nervous system and keep you centered.

Let go of the past. Getting out of your head and moving your focus from "what was" to "what is" will help you stay grounded and help you create more of what you want right now. Practice forgiving yourself and those who hurt you. Remain in the present by focusing on your breath.

Track your triggers. Understanding what irritates you and causes you anxiety is an important part of emotional self-care. When you're triggered, take a moment to figure out why and notice if there's a pattern. Jot it down, and from there, you can consciously learn to navigate and manage your impulses and emotions.

MOOD-BOOSTING RITUALS

Fire signs (Aries, Leo, Sagittarius): Learn to self-soothe. When your emotions become too big, learn how to self-regulate instead of impulsively reacting to those around you. Make yourself a comforting cup of tea, scream into a pillow, or distract yourself with a funny movie. Repeat affirmations like, "With each breath, I breathe in healing. I feel calmer, more relaxed, more self-confident," "I can rely on myself. I know I can handle tough times," and "I let go of all my fears and worries. I am safe."

Earth signs (Taurus, Virgo, Capricorn): Learn to lean on others and communicate openly. Embrace your vulnerability. Practice asking for help and support when you feel upset or need an extra hand. If you need space, that's okay. Instead of shutting out your inner circle, though, lovingly inform your loved ones that you need some alone time and you'll get back to them when you feel better. Repeat the mantras, "It is safe for me to express my true self," "I am accepted for who I am at all times," and "Vulnerability is my superpower."

Air signs (Gemini, Libra, Aquarius): Make time to feel. It's important for you to digest and feel what you're feeling rather than analyze or brush over your emotions. Carve out an hour or two each week to just be with yourself. See if there's any emotional residue that wants to move through you. Allow it to come out through tears or rage. Don't judge it or label it. Just feel it. Repeat the mantras, "I love me," "I am allowed to feel," and "It's okay to feel this way. Even though I feel this way, I am worthy of love and respect."

Water signs (Cancer, Scorpio, Pisces): Escape to the bathtub. To help ground your emotions, go to your safe haven: water. As a water sign, you're naturally drawn to its fluid calmness. Draw a warm bath and allow yourself to sit and honor your feelings and express them in whatever way they need to come out. The water will soothe you and bring you back to the present. Repeat these affirmations: "This too shall pass," "I am enough," and "It is safe to be me."

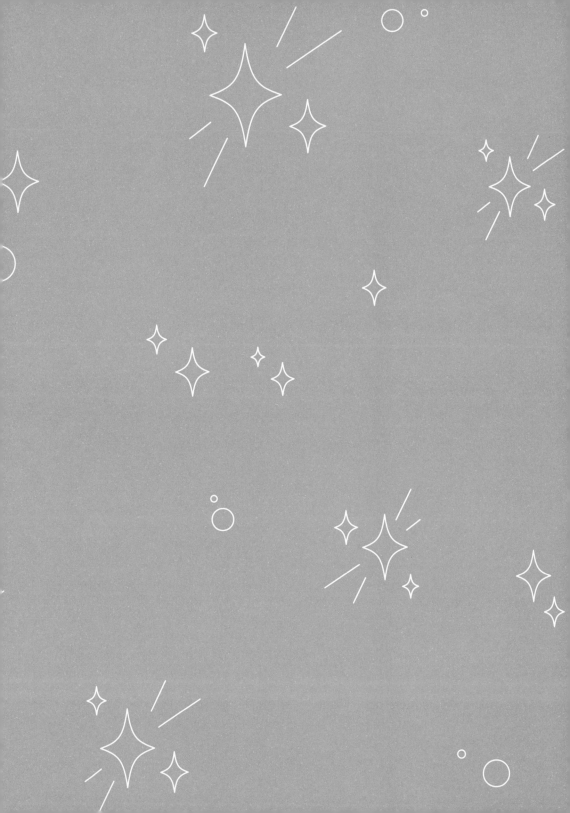

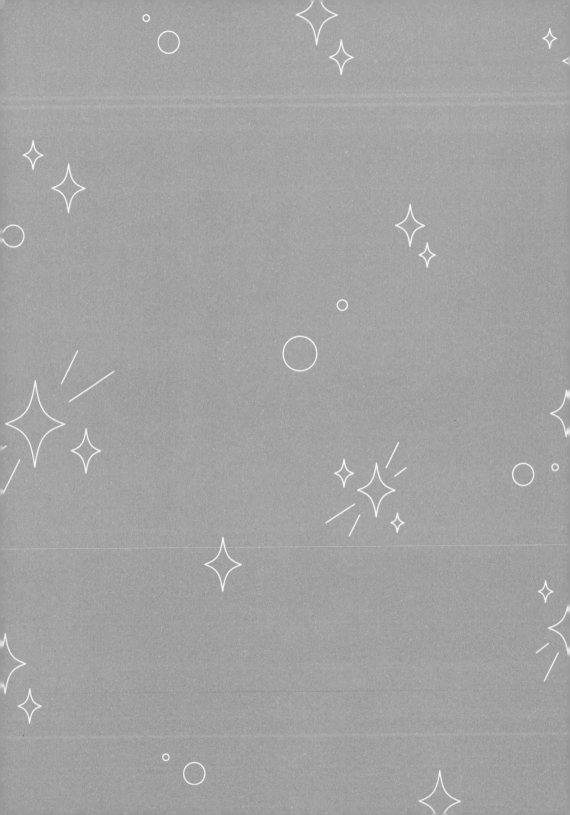